# Museums

Jennifer B. Gillis

**Rourke**

Publishing LLC

Vero Beach, Florida 32964

www.rourkepublishing.com

PHOTO CREDITS: All photos © Lynn M. Stone except pg. 5 © James P. Rowan

Editor: Robert Stengard-Olliges

Cover design by Michelle Moore.

imprint
TK

Dedication: The publisher would like to thank the following people for their expertise in the preparation of this book: Michelle Carr, Susan Lamb, Louise Benner, John Campbell, Robert Stone, and Glenn Bradshaw of the North Carolina Museum of History; Peggy Parks of the Children's Museum at Old Salem, North Carolina; Leiana Guerrero of the Museum of Life and Science, Durham, N.C.


**Library of Congress Cataloging-in-Publication Data**

Gillis, Jennifer Blizin, 1950-
 Museums : field trip / Jennifer Blizin Gillis.
     p. cm. --  (Field trips)
 Includes index.
 ISBN 978-1-60044-561-3
 1.  Museums--Juvenile literature.  I. Title.
 AM7.G54 2008
 069--dc22

                                        2007017255


Printed in the USA

CG/CG

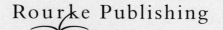

Rourke Publishing

www.rourkepublishing.com – rourke@rourkepublishing.com
Post Office Box 3328. Vero Beach. FL 32964

# Table of Contents

# Visiting a Museum

There are all kinds of museums. Some museums have **exhibits** about plants and animals. Others help us learn about history. There are museums for just about anything you can think of! Each museum may be different, but all museums are alike in some ways. They have **collections** of things for people to look at. There are signs and recordings that tell visitors about the exhibits.

Signs tell visitors about museum exhibits. ▶

# Who Will You Meet?

It takes many people to run a museum, so you may not meet all of them. An **educator** or **docent** may meet your class and explain the exhibits. You may see guards who protect the exhibits. You may meet the **curator** of a special exhibit.

A museum educator talks about the ▶ ancient saber tooth cat.

# Collecting Things

You may have a collection of baseball cards or dolls at home. How did you get those things? Museums get things the same way you do. Some people donate objects to museums as gifts. Sometimes museums borrow from other museums. Museums also buy items for their collections. Curators are always looking for new exhibits.

▲

Museums collect old things for new exhibits.

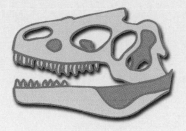

# Making an Exhibit

Museums only show some of their collection at a time. Curators spend a lot of time planning new exhibits. They have to decide what each new exhibit will be about and what will be in it. Artists and carpenters help design the exhibit.

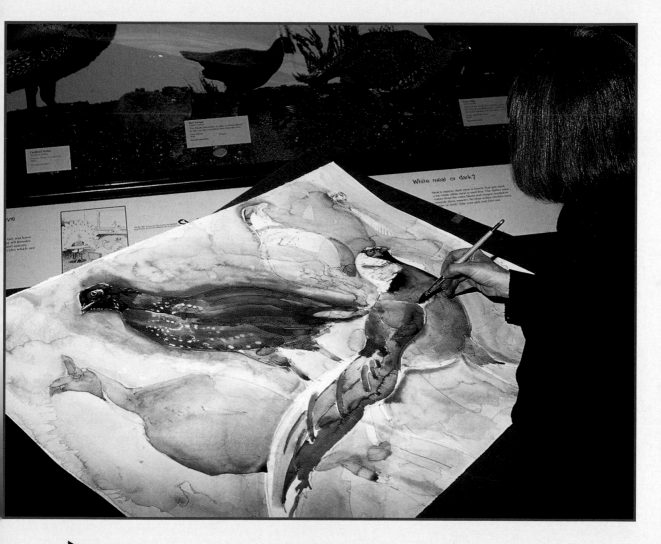

▶

A museum artist sketches ideas for a new exhibit.

# Learning about the Past

How did people dress in the old days? How did they live? You can find out in a history museum. Exhibits show how life changed over time. People who put the exhibits together must study history carefully so everything will look just as it would have in the past. Old items in a museum are called **artifacts**.

Old Barracks Museum in Trenton, New Jersey, ▶ shows artifacts and dressware of 1776.

Historic museums teach about the history of a town or a country. You can see old maps or pictures that show how a place used to look. There are often exhibits of old weapons or tools people used to make things. You may also see things people made long ago, such as pottery or baskets.

A Seminole museum displays old ▶ baskets, pottery, and weapons.

CORN SIFTING BASKETS

CORN SIFTING BASKETS

HUNTING BOW

15

STICK BALL GAME 'STICKS'

OT & SPOON

# Learning about Machines

Some museums show how jobs or machines have changed over time. It can be fun to look at old cars, farm machines, or **typewriters**. Some museums have **interactive** exhibits that let you hear what it was like to work in a factory or a mine. There are also museums where you can ride on old **trolleys** or trains.

A early diesel locomotive stands on a ▶ railway museum track.

# Learning about Science

Science museums teach about animals, the earth, and outer space. You may see bones from dinosaurs or other animals, or colorful rocks and minerals from deep inside the earth. There are interactive exhibits that help you understand the way things work.

This girl visiting a science museum is ▶ learning how the human heart works.

19

# Caring for Collections

Museum curators have to make sure their collections last for a long time. Light, heat, and the oil from people's skin can ruin artifacts. This is why visitors are not allowed to touch many exhibits. When museum workers have to clean or move things, they may wear special gloves.

A curator's assistant cleans a fish ▶ fossil in a museum lab.

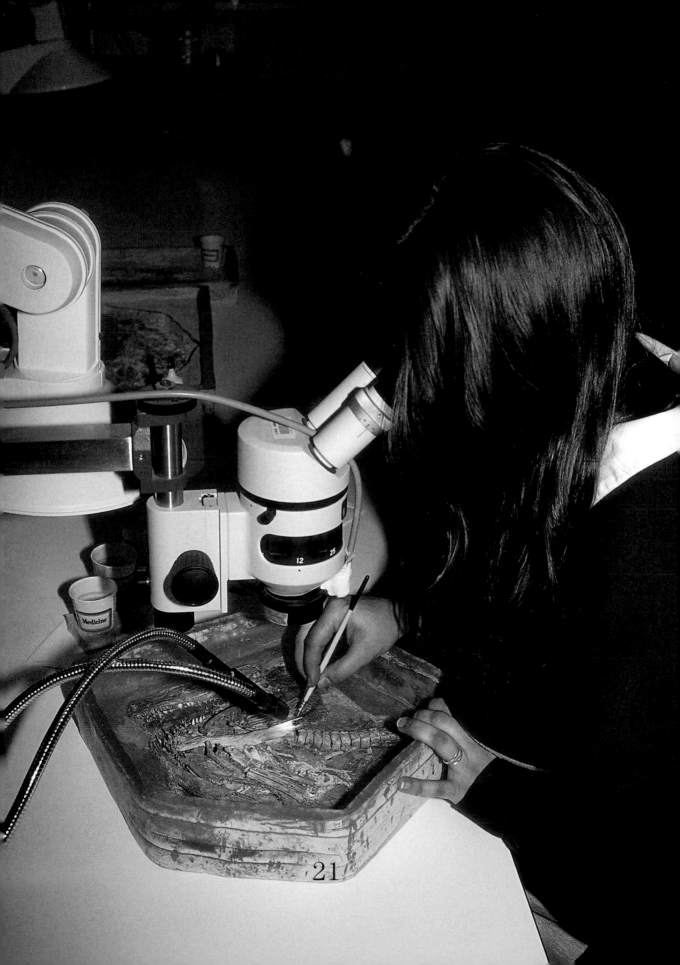

# Did You Know?

- If it seems dark inside museums, that's because it is! Sunlight can damage artifacts, so museums do not have many windows.

- If you can't visit a museum, sometimes the museum can visit you. Many museums have traveling exhibits that go to schools or libraries.

- There are museums for just about anything you can think of. You can see exhibits of instruments and clothing from famous musicians at the Rock n' Roll Hall of Fame in Ohio. In Paris, France, you can learn about the history of the sewers at the Sewer Museum. You can see George Washington's false teeth at the Museum of Dentistry in Baltimore, Maryland.

- Many museums have summer camps where you can spend a week or more learning about the exhibits in detail.

# Glossary

**artifact** (AR te fact) — something left over from the past

**collection** (kuh LEK shun) — group of things owned by a museum

**curator** (KYOOR ay ter) — person who collects, studies, and cares for artifacts in a museum

**docent** (DOH sent) — someone who volunteers in a museum and who is not paid

**educator** (EJ you kate r) — person at a museum, planetarium, or other public place who teaches people about the exhibits

**exhibit** (eg ZIB it) — something put in a place where many people can see it

**interactive** (in ter AK tiv) — an exhibit in a museum in which a visitor pushes a button or another activity that makes something happen in the exhibit

**trolley** (TROLL ee) — vehicle something like a bus that runs on a track and runs on electricity

**typewriter** (TIPE ry ter) — machine that can print letters on paper when certain keys are pressed

# Index

## Further Reading

Lehman, Barbara. *Museum Trip*. Houghton Mifflin, 2006.
Lilly, Alexandra. *Holocaust Museum*. Compass Point Books, 2007.
Trenc, Milan. *The Night at the Museum*. Barrons, 2007.

## Websites to Visit

www.si.edu/museums
www.bostonchildrensmuseum.org
www.amnh.org

## About the Author

Jennifer B. Gillis is an author and editor of nonfiction books and poetry for children. A graduate of Gilford College in North Carolina, she has taught foreign language and social studies in North Carolina, Virginia, and Illinois.